RUNNERS

Written by
M.L. Matthews

Illustrated by
Jamar Whiteside

Order this book online at www.trafford.com
or email orders@trafford.com

Most Trafford titles are also available at major online book retailers.

© Copyright 2011 M. L. Matthews.

All rights reserved. No part of this publication may be reproduced, stored in a retrieval system, or transmitted, in any form or by any means, electronic, mechanical, photocopying, recording, or otherwise, without the written prior permission of the author.

Printed in the United States of America.

ISBN: 978-1-4269-7575-2

Library of Congress Control Number: 2011912342

Trafford rev. 08/11/2011

   www.trafford.com

North America & international
toll-free: 1 888 232 4444 (USA & Canada)
phone: 250 383 6864 ♦ fax: 812 355 4082

RUNNERS

Written by
M.L. Matthews

Illustrated by
Jamar Whiteside

Translated by
Kiara Rainey

Some runners run for fortune.

Some runners run for fame.

Some run because they love to run.

They are all runners just the same.

Unos corredores corren por la fortuna.

Unos corredores corren por la fama.

Unos corren porque les encanta correr.

Todos son corredores de la misma.

Little girls run and so do little boys.

So they can stay happy, they think about their toys.

Some runners are millionaires. Others are unemployed.

Jose runs around mountains. So does Mr. Boyd.

Las ninas corren y los ninos tambien.

Para estar contentos, ellos piensan en sus juguetes.

Unos corredores son millonarios. Otros están desempleados.

Jose corre alrededor de montanas y Sr. Boyd tambien.

Artists run with pictures they have drawn.

Some runners run from dusk to dawn.

Chess players run with kings and pawns.

Runners run, not just stand on the lawn.

Artistas corren con dibujos que han dibujado.

Unos corren de anochecer a alba.

Jugadores de ajedrez corren con los reyes y peones.

Corredores corren, no sólo están de pie en el césped.

There are runners with short legs and long legs too.
Some are running before the roosters say cock-a-doodle-doo.
Each and every runner does the best that they could do.
Runners must stay focused on the goals that they pursue.

Hay corredores con piernas chicas y piernas largas, tambien.

Unos corren antes de que los gallos digan qui-qui-ri-quí.

Cada corredor hace lo mejor que puede hacer.

Corredores deben quedarse enfocados en las metas que ellos persiguen.

Runners run with wind in their faces.

They run through smelly places.

Runners run at different paces.

Some run with no shoe laces.

Corredores corren con el viento en sus caras.

Corren por lugares con olores malos.

Corredores corren en pasos diferentes.

Unos corren sin cintas en los zapatos.

Some run with their dogs while others run with their cats.

Some run wearing jackets. Others run wearing hats.

Basketball players dribble and run.

Baseball players run with their bats.

Unos corren con sus perros mientras otros corren con sus gatos.

Unos corren con chaquetas. Otros corren con sombreros.

Jugadores de baloncesto botan el balon y corren.

Jugadores de beisbol corren con sus bates de beisbol.

Tall runners run and short runners too.

They run past the markets and even by the zoo.

Some run in packs of four, three, or two.

Some packs run with packs to make a whole slew.

Corredores altos corren y corredores chaparros tambien.

Corren pasando por los mercados y por el zoologico.

Unos corren en grupos de cuatro, tres, o dos.

Unos grupos corren con otros grupos para crear un grupo grandisimo.

Keosha runs and so does Jack.

Some runners live in mansions. Some runners live in shacks.

Runners give back, but don't look back.

Runners focus on what is ahead. That's where the prize is at.

Keosha corre y Jack corre, tambien.

Unos corredores viven en casas grandes. Unos corredores viven en casas pequeñas.

Corredores donan, pero no miran detras.

Corredores se concentran en lo que esta delante. Esto es donde el premio está.

Runners run when it's breezy.

Running is not always easy.

Runners cough and get wheezy.

Some runners run until their stomachs are queasy.

Los corredores corren cuando es ventoso.

Correr no es siempre facil.

Corredores tosen y se hacen sibilantes.

Unos corredores corren hasta que sus estomagos sean delicados.

We are the runners running under the sun.

We run for shelter when the strong winds come.

There is no time to delay for the race has begun.

If you haven't started yet, then get up and run!

Somos los corredores que corren bajo el sol.

Corremos al refugio cuando los vientos fuertes vienen.

No hay tiempo para perder porque la carrera ha comenzado.

!Si no has empezado todavia, entonces levantate y corre!

www.ingramcontent.com/pod-product-compliance
Lightning Source LLC
Chambersburg PA
CBHW042303060426
42446CB00039B/215